LEADERS LIKE US

Oscar de la Renta

BY ANNETTE M. CLAYTON

ILLUSTRATED BY ELISA CHAVARRI

Rourke

Before Reading: *Building Background Knowledge and Vocabulary*

Building background knowledge can help children process new information and build upon what they already know. Before reading a book, it is important to tap into what children already know about the topic. This will help them develop their vocabulary and increase their reading comprehension.

Questions and Activities to Build Background Knowledge:

1. Look at the front cover of the book and read the title. What do you think this book will be about?
2. What do you already know about this topic?
3. Take a book walk and skim the pages. Look at the table of contents, photographs, captions, and bold words. Did these text features give you any information or predictions about what you will read in this book?

Vocabulary: *Vocabulary Is Key to Reading Comprehension*

Use the following directions to prompt a conversation about each word.

- Read the vocabulary words.
- What comes to mind when you see each word?
- What do you think each word means?

Vocabulary Words:
- designer
- elegant
- empire
- fashionable
- immigrated
- interviewed
- launch
- sketch

During Reading: *Reading for Meaning and Understanding*

To achieve deep comprehension of a book, children are encouraged to use close reading strategies. During reading, it is important to have children stop and make connections. These connections result in deeper analysis and understanding of a book.

Close Reading a Text

During reading, have children stop and talk about the following:

- Any confusing parts
- Any unknown words
- Text to text, text to self, text to world connections
- The main idea in each chapter or heading

Encourage children to use context clues to determine the meaning of any unknown words. These strategies will help children learn to analyze the text more thoroughly as they read.

When you are finished reading this book, turn to the next-to-last page for **Text-Dependent Questions** and an **Extension Activity**.

TABLE OF CONTENTS

A WORLD OF ART

Have you ever had a dream that seemed impossible? Oscar de la Renta loved clothing and art. He wanted to be a famous fashion **designer**. But he was from the Dominican Republic. Successful designers were usually French or Italian. But Oscar worked hard and never gave up. He built a fashion **empire**.

Oscar thumbed through fabrics on the shelf. He was designing a dress for a client. It needed to be finished soon, but Oscar was stuck. He closed his eyes and thought of the Dominican Republic, the sunny island where he grew up. He pictured a rainbow of colors—rose pink, mango orange, and crystal blue water. He began to **sketch**. To Oscar, the whole world was art.

A QUICK STUDY

At eighteen, Oscar left the Dominican Republic and traveled to Spain to study painting. While there, he worked as an illustrator for fashion designers. He spent many days sketching clothes. The world of fashion lit a spark inside Oscar. He left painting behind and moved on to his new passion—designing clothes.

Soon, he traveled to Paris, the most **fashionable** city in the world.

He **interviewed** with a famous fashion designer, Antonio del Castillo. He looked over Oscar's sketches. They were very good! Castillo asked Oscar if he knew how to sew clothing.

Oscar gulped. He didn't. But he shook his head and said yes. Castillo hired Oscar on the spot.

Heart pounding, Oscar raced to a French fashion school. He told the head teacher what happened. Oscar asked if she could teach him a year's worth of sewing in two weeks. Luckily, she said yes.

Under Castillo's mentorship, Oscar designed custom-made clothing.

In 1962, First Lady Jackie Kennedy Onassis wore a dress designed by Oscar. That set off a tradition of Oscar designing clothes for first ladies.

The next year, Oscar **immigrated** to America. He landed a job at the fashion house Elizabeth Arden, designing gowns. His style continued to gain popularity.

WHITE HOUSE GOWNS

Oscar designed gowns for many first ladies. This includes Nancy Reagan, Hillary Clinton, Laura Bush, and Michelle Obama.

A CUT ABOVE THE REST

In 1965, Oscar decided it was time to **launch** his own clothing line. He drew inspiration from the bright flowers that bloomed in his home country. He was also inspired by art, history, and different cultures. Oscar's dresses became very successful. He didn't want women to just look beautiful, he wanted them to feel beautiful too.

His designs featured silky skirts...

...brilliant florals...

...and endless elegance.

Oscar's ballgowns were known for being **elegant** and flowery. But in the 1980s, Oscar saw the world change. Where it used to be the very rich influencing fashion and trends, Oscar began to see working women as the height of fashion influence. He wanted to dress these powerful individuals. He began designing chic business suits for women. These suits helped women feel powerful and elegant at the same time.

POWER SUITS

Oscar's suits for women were known for their bold colors. First lady Hillary Clinton wore many of them during her time in the White House and later as a state senator.

Over the years, Oscar's gowns floated down the red carpet. Some of the biggest names in the world have worn his dresses to award shows, parties, and movie premieres.

Rihanna

Taylor Swift

19

Oscar devoted his life to fashion, but was also very kind and generous. He donated money to open La Casa del Niño in the Dominican Republic. The center cares for over 1,500 children every day. Those who knew him best describe Oscar as warm, funny, and a gentleman. Oscar passed away at age 82 in 2014. Through his clothing and charitable giving, Oscar's legacy lives on.

> Fashion is about dressing according to what's fashionable. Style is more about being yourself.
>
> - Oscar de la Renta

TIME LINE

1932   Oscar de la Renta is born on July 22 in Santo Domingo, Dominican Republic.

1950   Oscar studies painting at the Royal Academy of Fine Arts in Spain.

1963   Oscar becomes an American citizen but retains his citizenship in the Dominican Republic.

1964   Oscar's designs appear in *Vogue* magazine.

1969   Oscar receives the Neiman Marcus Fashion Award for distinguished service in the field of fashion.

1973   Oscar is named President of the Council of Fashion Designers of America (CFDA).

1977   Oscar launches his first perfume fragrance, Oscar.

1982   Oscar helps open La Casa del Niño in the Dominican Republic for underprivileged children.

1989   Oscar receives the CFDA lifetime achievement award.

1998   First Lady Hillary Clinton posed for the cover of *Vogue* magazine wearing one of Oscar's dresses.

2005   Oscar designs an inauguration gown for First Lady Laura Bush.

2006   Oscar launches a bridal gown collection.

2014   First Lady Michelle Obama wears a dress designed by Oscar de la Renta.

2014   On October 20, Oscar passes away from cancer.

GLOSSARY

designer (di-ZYE-nur): a person who designs something, such as clothing, especially as a job

elegant (EL-uh-guhnt): graceful and pleasing to look at

empire (EM-pire): a large organization or company controlled by one person

fashionable (FASH-uh-nuh-buhl): liked by many people during a particular time

immigrated (im-i-GRAY-ted): to have come to another country to live permanently

interviewed (IN-tur-vyood): meeting with someone about a job

launch (lawnch): to introduce something new

sketch (skech): a quick rough drawing without much detail

INDEX

TEXT-DEPENDENT QUESTIONS

1. What did Oscar first study while in Spain?
2. Name one thing that inspired Oscar's clothing designs.
3. Why did Oscar begin designing suits for women in the 1980s?
4. Name a first lady that wore a dress by Oscar de la Renta.

EXTENSION ACTIVITY

Imagine you are designing an outfit for your favorite celebrity, musician, athlete, or hero. What would you use for inspiration? What unique features would make it your signature style?

ABOUT THE AUTHOR

Annette M. Clayton is an author living in Maryland with her husband, twin daughters, and one fluffy cat. She hopes to share stories that will inspire children's imaginations, spark creativity, and foster inclusivity. For fun, she likes to hike, visit Disney World, or read a good book. To learn more about her, visit her at www.AnnetteMClayton.com.

ABOUT THE ILLUSTRATOR

Elisa Chavarri is an award-winning illustrator who strives to create work that inspires happiness, promotes inclusiveness and curiosity, and helps people of all different backgrounds feel special. She has illustrated numerous books for children including the Pura Belpré Honor book *Sharuko: El Arqueólogo Peruano/Peruvian Archaeologist Julio C. Tello*. Elisa hails from Lima, Peru, and resides in Alpena, Michigan, with her husband and two young children.

www.rourkebooks.com

PHOTO CREDITS: page 20: ZUMA Press, Inc. / Alamy Stock Photo

Quote source: Heilpern, John. "The Importance of Being Oscar." *Vanity Fair*, Aug. 13, 2009, https://www.vanityfair.com/news/2009/09/out-to-lunch-de-la-renta200909.

Edited by: Hailey Scragg
Illustrations by: Elisa Chavarri
Cover and interior layout by: J.J. Giddings

Library of Congress PCN Data

Oscar de la Renta/ Annette M. Clayton
(Leaders Like Us)
ISBN 978-1-73165-772-5 (hard cover) (alk. paper)
ISBN 978-1-73165-774-9 (soft cover)
ISBN 978-1-73165-776-3 (e-book)
ISBN 978-1-73165-778-7 (e-pub)
Library of Congress Control Number: 2023942369

Rourke Educational Media
Printed in the United States of America
01-0152411937